after-school food

after-school food

Tempting and nutritious recipes for your child

Love Food ™ is an imprint of Parragon Books Ltd.

Parragon
Queen Street House
4 Queen Street
Bath BA1 1HE, UK

ISBN 978-1-4075-0245-8

Printed in China

Designed by Fiona Roberts
Introduction text by Beverly LeBlanc
Photography by Mike Cooper
Cover Models: Carly Lou, Harry and Tilly Glass

NOTES FOR THE READER
This book uses both metric and imperial measurements. Follow the same units of measurement
throughout; do not mix metric and imperial. All spoon measurements are level; teaspoons are assumed
to be 5 ml and tablespoons are assumed to be 15 ml. Unless otherwise stated, milk is assumed to be
whole, individual vegetables such as potatoes are medium, and pepper is freshly ground black pepper.
Recipes using raw or very lightly cooked eggs should be avoided by children, the elderly, pregnant
women, convalescents, and anyone suffering from an illness. Pregnant and breastfeeding women are
also advised to avoid eating peanuts and peanut products. The times given are an approximate
guide only. Preparation times differ according to the techniques used by different
people and the cooking times may also vary from those given.

contents

Introduction

As every parent or carer knows, it is a challenge to get young school children to eat healthily. But it is a challenge worth accepting, because if they develop good eating habits at an early age, they will reap benefits throughout their adult lives.

The greater variety of foods your children eat every day, the more likely they are to get all the essential vitamins and minerals they need for their growing and developing bodies. And what your children eat when they come home hungry from school can have long-lasting effects. Try substituting Hummus with Crunchy Vegetables (see page 24) for a packet of crisps, and get your children into the habit of eating healthy snacks.

Eating Well for Life

High-profile campaigns have highlighted the important role a healthy diet plays in everything from children's overall health and behaviour to their concentration and performance in the classroom. Ideally, their diet – like your diet – should include plenty of fruit and vegetables, cereals, rice, pasta, bread and potatoes, with small amounts of lean meat, poultry, fish, eggs and pulses.

Foods high in fat, sugar and salt should only be eaten occasionally, and as youngsters' leisure time activities move from the playground to the computer, obesity is increasing at an alarming rate. Ways to counter this trend include offering water or milk instead of sweetened fizzy drinks, and fruit and vegetables rather than sugary biscuits and cakes – save those for occasional treats, rather than everyday snacks.

Yet actually getting kids to eat food that is good for them is easier said than done. Most children will choose a packet of crisps over crudités every day of the week, and school-aged children are notoriously fussy eaters. *After-school Food,* however, can help you achieve your goal with yummy, healthy recipes that make snacks and mealtimes pleasurable.

Strong Bones!

School-aged children need a variety of vitamins and minerals every day for optimum health, and calcium is a particularly important nutrient, as it is essential for healthy bones and teeth. Whole milk, yogurt and small amounts of cheese are all excellent sources. Or try desserts such as Mini Strawberry Cheesecakes (see page 86) and Chocolate Mousse Pots (see page 82) – they will be hard to resist!

Go for 5

We are all encouraged to eat five portions of fruit and vegetables every day, because they are such a good source of vitamins, minerals and fibre. But as most parents know, getting children to eat one portion, let alone five, is not easy. You'll find imaginative ideas for incorporating vegetables into tasty main courses in the Vegetable Delights chapter, beginning on page 52. And don't forget tempting yet healthy desserts, such as Fruit Skewers (see page 94).

Setting an Example

Always remember young children learn by copying adults, so the best way to encourage healthy eating is for you to choose the healthy options and set regular mealtimes. Mix and match recipes in the Meat, Poultry & Fish Feasts (see page 30) and Vegetable Delights chapters, and the whole family will benefit.

chapter 1

Super Snacks

Creamy Tomato Soup

serves 4

1 tbsp butter
½ red onion, minced
1 leek, chopped
1 garlic clove, crushed
1 carrot, peeled and grated
1 potato, peeled and grated
300 ml / 10 fl oz low-salt
  vegetable stock
500 g / 1 lb 2 oz ripe tomatoes, peeled,
  deseeded and chopped
1 tbsp tomato purée
salt and pepper
150 ml / 5 fl oz full-fat milk
snipped chives, to garnish (optional)
Granary rolls, to serve

Melt the butter in a large saucepan over a low heat and cook the onion, leek and garlic for 10 minutes, or until very soft but not browned.

Add the carrot and potato and cook for 5 minutes. Add the stock and bring up to simmering point.

Add the tomatoes and tomato purée and season to taste with salt and pepper. Simmer for 15 minutes until the vegetables are very soft. Add the milk and warm through, then transfer the soup to a blender or food processor and process until very smooth. You can pass the soup through a sieve at this stage, if you like.

Return the soup to the rinsed-out saucepan and reheat gently. Pour into warmed serving bowls and garnish the soup with the snipped chives, if desired. Serve with Granary rolls.

Hearty Bean & Pasta Soup

serves 4

4 tbsp olive oil

1 onion, finely chopped

1 celery stick, chopped

1 carrot, peeled and diced

1 bay leaf

1.2 litres / 2 pints low-salt
   vegetable stock

400 g / 14 oz can chopped tomatoes

175 g / 6 oz pasta shapes, such as
   farfalle, shells or twists

400 g / 14 oz can cannellini beans,
   drained and rinsed

salt and pepper

200 g / 7 oz spinach or chard, thick
   stalks removed and shredded

40 g / 1½ oz Parmesan cheese,
   finely grated

Heat the olive oil in a large, heavy-based saucepan. Add the onion, celery and carrot and cook over a medium heat for 8–10 minutes, stirring occasionally, until the vegetables have softened.

Add the bay leaf, stock and chopped tomatoes, then bring to the boil. Reduce the heat, cover and simmer for 15 minutes, or until the vegetables are just tender.

Add the pasta and beans, then bring the soup back to the boil and cook for 10 minutes, or until the pasta is just tender. Stir occasionally to prevent the pasta sticking to the bottom of the pan and burning.

Season to taste, add the spinach and cook for a further 2 minutes, or until tender. Serve, sprinkled with Parmesan cheese.

Chicken & Apple Bites

makes 20

1 apple, peeled, cored and grated

2 skinless, boneless chicken breasts,
  cut into chunks

½ red onion, finely chopped

1 tbsp finely chopped fresh parsley

50 g/1¼ oz fresh wholemeal
  breadcrumbs

1 tbsp concentrated chicken stock

wholemeal flour, for coating

groundnut oil, for shallow-frying

Spread the apple out on a clean tea towel and press out all the excess moisture.

Put the chicken, apple, onion, parsley, breadcrumbs and stock in a food processor and pulse briefly until well combined.

Spread the flour out on a plate. Divide the mixture into 20 mini portions, shape each portion into a ball and roll in the flour.

Heat a little oil in a non-stick frying pan over a medium heat and cook the balls for 5–8 minutes, or until golden brown all over and cooked through. Remove and drain on kitchen paper. Serve hot or cold.

Chive Scrambled Eggs with Brioche

serves 2

4 eggs

100 ml / 3½ fl oz single cream

salt and pepper

*2 tbsp snipped fresh chives, plus 4 whole
    fresh chives to garnish*

25 g / 1 oz butter

4 slices brioche loaf, lightly toasted

Break the eggs into a medium bowl and whisk gently with the cream. Season to taste with salt and pepper and add the snipped chives.

Melt the butter in a sauté pan and pour in the egg mixture. Leave to set slightly, then move the mixture towards the centre of the pan using a wooden spoon as the eggs begin to cook. Continue in this way until the eggs are cooked but still creamy.

Place the toasted brioche slices in the centre of 2 plates and spoon over the scrambled eggs. Serve immediately, garnished with whole chives.

Tortillas with Tuna, Egg & Sweetcorn

serves 2

1 large egg, hard-boiled and cooled

200 g / 7 oz canned tuna in spring
    water, drained

200 g / 7 oz canned no-added-sugar
    sweetcorn kernels, drained

2 wholemeal flour tortillas

1 punnet mustard cress

dressing

1 tbsp natural yogurt

1 tsp olive oil

$\frac{1}{2}$ tsp white wine vinegar

$\frac{1}{2}$ tsp Dijon mustard

pepper

To make the dressing, whisk the yogurt, oil, vinegar and mustard, and pepper to taste, in a jug until emulsified and smooth.

Shell the egg, separate the yolk and the white, then mash the yolk and chop the white finely. Mash the tuna with the egg and dressing, then mix in the sweetcorn.

Spread the filling equally over the 2 tortillas and sprinkle over the mustard cress. Fold in one end and roll up.

Cheese Twists

makes 20 twists

butter or margarine, for greasing

85 g / 3 oz Gruyère cheese, grated

½ tsp paprika

375 g / 13 oz ready-rolled puff pastry,
defrosted if frozen

1 egg, beaten

Preheat the oven to 200°C/400°F/Gas Mark 6. Grease a large baking sheet.

Mix together the Gruyère cheese and paprika and sprinkle over the sheet of puff pastry. Fold the puff pastry in half and roll out a little to seal the edges.

Cut the pastry into long 1-cm/½-inch wide strips, then cut each strip in half and gently twist. Place on the prepared baking sheet. Brush with the beaten egg and bake for 10–12 minutes, or until crisp and golden. Allow to cool on a wire rack.

Avocado Dip with Spicy Potato Skins

serves 6–8

4 large baking potatoes, scrubbed

3 tbsp olive oil

1 garlic clove, crushed

¼ tsp paprika

½ tsp dried chilli flakes (optional)

salt and pepper

avocado dip

2 ripe avocados, stoned and peeled

juice of ½ lemon

150 g/5½ oz soft goat's cheese

Preheat the oven to 190°C/375°F/Gas Mark 5. Rub the potatoes with 1 tablespoon of the oil, place on a baking sheet and bake in the preheated oven for 1–1½ hours, or until the flesh is soft.

Remove the potatoes from the oven, cut in half lengthways and carefully scoop out the flesh into a bowl, but leave a generous 1 cm/½ inch of the potato on the skins. You can use the potato flesh to make mash.

Cut the skins into wedges. Put the remaining oil in a large bowl with the garlic, paprika and chilli flakes, if using, and mix until well combined. Season sparingly with salt and pepper.

Toss the potato wedges in the spicy oil, spread out on the baking sheet and bake in the oven for 20 minutes until the skins are brown and crisp.

Meanwhile make the dip. In a separate bowl mash the avocado with the lemon juice, then mash in the cheese and a little of the potato flesh until well combined and smooth.

Serve the spicy skins warm, piled up, with little pots of the dip.

Hummus with Crunchy Vegetables

makes 10 portions

*200 g / 7 oz no-salt, no-sugar canned
    chickpeas, drained and rinsed*
½ garlic clove, crushed
3 tbsp tahini
freshly squeezed lemon juice, to taste
1 tbsp natural yogurt
*carrot sticks, red pepper sticks, cucumber
    sticks and apple wedges, to serve*

Place the chickpeas in a blender with the garlic, tahini, lemon juice and yogurt. Blend until smooth.

Store in the refrigerator for up to 3 days and serve with carrot sticks, red pepper sticks, cucumber sticks and apple wedges.

Mini Pizzas

makes 6

3 wholemeal English muffins, halved

2 tbsp tomato purée

2 tbsp pesto

1 tbsp olive oil

$\frac{1}{2}$ red onion, thinly sliced

3 mushrooms, sliced

$\frac{1}{2}$ courgette, thinly sliced

2–3 slices ham or 6 slices salami

100 g / 3$\frac{1}{2}$ oz grated Cheddar cheese or
    6 slices mozzarella cheese

Toast the muffins until golden, then leave to cool.

Mix the tomato purée and pesto together in a small bowl and spread equally over the muffin halves.

Heat the oil in a non-stick frying pan and then cook the onion, mushrooms and courgette until soft and beginning to brown.

Preheat the grill to high. Divide the vegetables between the muffins and top with the ham and then the cheese.

Cook under the grill for 3–4 minutes until the cheese is melted and browned. Serve hot or cold.

Grilled Cheese Sandwich

serves 4

1 stoneground buckwheat boule loaf
(about 17.5 cm / 7 inch diameter) or
other rustic round loaf

175 g / 6 oz Cheddar cheese, finely
shaved or coarsely grated

1 large avocado, halved, stoned, peeled
and sliced

2 tomatoes, halved and cut into fine wedges

12 asparagus spears, cooked, bottled
or canned

4 slices Parma, Serrano or Black Forest ham

pepper

olive oil

Slice the crusty top off the loaf; reserve for another use. Slice the loaf into two layers, making the bottom thicker. Place the bottom on a large piece of cooking foil.

Preheat the grill on the hottest setting. Toast the top surface of the top layer of the loaf until brown, then turn it and place on the foil.

Sprinkle 100 g of cheese over both layers of bread. Arrange the avocado and tomato wedges on the bottom layer then sprinkle with half the remaining cheese. Top with the asparagus spears and ham, completely covering the edges of the ingredients underneath. Sprinkle with the remaining cheese and a trickle of olive oil.

Cook well away from the heat source for 3–5 minutes. Remove the plain cheese-topped layer first, when the cheese is bubbling. Cook the bottom layer until the cheese has melted and the ham is browned.

Cut the toasted cheese layer into 8 wedges and overlap them on the filling, alternating the plain and cheese sides up. Serve at once, cut into four wedges.

chapter 2

Meat, Poultry & Fish Feasts

Home-made Chicken Nuggets

serves 4

3 skinless, boneless chicken breasts

4 tbsp wholemeal plain flour

1 tbsp wheatgerm

½ tsp ground cumin

½ tsp ground coriander

pepper

1 egg, lightly beaten

2 tbsp olive oil

dipping sauce

100 g / 3½ oz sunblush tomatoes

100 g / 3½ oz fresh tomatoes, peeled,
*   deseeded and chopped*

2 tbsp mayonnaise

Preheat the oven to 190°C/375°F/Gas Mark 5. Cut the chicken breasts into 4-cm/1½-inch chunks. Mix the flour, wheatgerm, cumin, coriander, and pepper to taste, in a bowl, then divide in half and put on 2 separate plates. Put the beaten egg on a third plate.

Pour the oil into a baking tray and heat in the oven. Roll the chicken pieces in one plate of flour, shake to remove any excess, then roll in the egg and finally in the second plate of flour, again shaking off any excess flour. When all the nuggets are ready, remove the baking tray from the oven and toss the nuggets in the hot oil. Roast in the oven for 25–30 minutes until golden and crisp.

Meanwhile, to make the dipping sauce, put both kinds of tomatoes in a blender or food processor and process until smooth. Add the mayonnaise and process again until well combined.

Remove the nuggets from the oven and drain on kitchen paper. Serve with the dipping sauce.

Sunny Rice

serves 4

450 g / 1 lb undyed smoked haddock or
    cod fillets
225 g / 8 oz basmati rice, rinsed
450 ml / 16 fl oz water
1 bay leaf
2 cloves
4 tbsp butter
55 g / 2 oz frozen petit pois
1 tsp garam masala
½ tsp ground turmeric
pepper
2 tbsp chopped flat-leaf parsley
4 hard-boiled eggs, quartered

Put the haddock in a large frying pan and pour enough milk or water over the fish to just cover it. Poach the fish for 5 minutes or until cooked and opaque. Remove the haddock from the pan and flake the fish, carefully removing the skin and any bones. Discard the remainder of the poaching liquid.

Meanwhile, place the rice in a saucepan and cover with 475 ml / 16 fl oz water then add the bay leaf and cloves. Bring to the boil, then reduce the heat and simmer, covered, for 15 minutes or until the water has been absorbed and the rice is tender. Discard the bay leaf and cloves. Set aside the covered pan.

Melt the butter over a gentle heat in the cleaned frying pan, then add the peas and cook for 2 minutes, or until tender. Stir in the garam masala and turmeric and cook for another minute.

Stir in the haddock and rice and mix well until they are coated in the spiced butter.

Season with pepper and heat through for 1–2 minutes. Stir in the parsley and top with the hard-boiled eggs just before serving.

Sticky Drumsticks & Cucumber Salad

serves 6

6 chicken drumsticks

2 tbsp maple syrup

2 tbsp low-salt soy sauce

1 tsp sesame oil

½ cucumber, thinly sliced

salt

2 spring onions, thinly sliced

Preheat the oven to 190°C/375°F/Gas Mark 5. Trim the chicken drumsticks of any excess skin and pat dry with kitchen paper.

Mix the maple syrup, soy sauce and sesame oil in a large bowl. Add the chicken drumsticks and toss well to coat.

Place the chicken drumsticks on a non-stick baking sheet and roast in the preheated oven for 30–40 minutes, basting occasionally, until the chicken is tender, well browned and sticky, and the juices run clear when a skewer is inserted into the thickest part of the meat.

Meanwhile, put the cucumber in a colander and sprinkle with a little salt. Leave for 10 minutes until the juices have drained out. Pat dry with kitchen paper and mix with the spring onions.

Serve the chicken hot or cold with the cucumber salad.

Shepherd's Pie

serves 4

2 tbsp olive oil

750 g / 1 lb 10 oz lean fresh lamb mince

1 leek, chopped

1 small red onion, finely chopped

2 carrots, chopped

1 celery stick, chopped

100 g / 3½ oz mushrooms, chopped

400 g / 14 oz canned tomatoes

2 tbsp fresh thyme leaves

125 ml / 4 fl oz water

salt and pepper

500 g / 1 lb 2 oz potatoes, boiled and mashed

400 g / 14 oz sweet potatoes, boiled and mashed

4 tbsp milk

knob of unsalted butter

Heat half the oil in a non-stick frying pan and cook the mince over a high heat, breaking it up with a wooden spoon, until well browned. Remove the mince from the pan with a slotted spoon, pour away any fat and wipe the pan with kitchen paper.

Add the remaining oil to the frying pan and cook the leek, onion, carrots and celery for 15 minutes until soft. Return the mince to the pan and add the mushrooms, tomatoes, thyme and water. Season to taste with salt and pepper and leave to simmer for 40 minutes, stirring occasionally.

Meanwhile, preheat the oven to 180°C / 350°F / Gas Mark 4. Mix the 2 mashes of potatoes with half the milk and half the butter in a bowl and season to taste with salt and pepper.

Spoon the meat sauce into a baking dish and top with the potato mixture. Brush with the remaining milk and dot with the remaining butter. Bake in the preheated oven for 35 minutes until the topping is brown and crisp.

Spaghetti Bolognese

serves 4

350 g / 12 oz spaghetti or pasta of
your choice

bolognese sauce

2 tbsp olive oil
1 onion, finely chopped
2 garlic cloves, finely chopped
1 carrot, peeled and finely chopped
85 g / 3 oz mushrooms, peeled and sliced
or chopped (optional)
1 tsp dried oregano
½ tsp dried thyme
1 bay leaf
280 g / 10 oz lean mince
300 ml / 10 fl oz stock
300 ml / 10 fl oz passata
pepper
grated Parmesan cheese, for sprinkling
(optional)

To make the sauce, heat the oil in a heavy-based, non-stick saucepan. Add the onion and sauté, half covered, for 5 minutes, or until softened. Add the garlic, carrot and mushrooms, if using, and sauté for a further 3 minutes, stirring occasionally.

Add the herbs and mince to the pan and cook until the meat has browned, stirring regularly.

Add the stock and passata. Reduce the heat, season to taste and cook over a medium-low heat, half covered, for 15–20 minutes, or until the sauce has reduced and thickened. Remove the bay leaf.

Meanwhile, cook the pasta according to the instructions on the packet, until the pasta is tender. Drain well and mix together the pasta and sauce until the pasta is well coated. Serve immediately, sprinkled with the grated Parmesan cheese, if liked.

Bacon, Pea & Potato Frittata

serves 3–4

2–3 slices good-quality bacon
1½ tbsp olive oil
1 small onion, finely chopped
350 g / 12 oz new potatoes, cooked,
    halved or quartered, if large
55 g / 2 oz frozen petit pois
6 free range eggs, lightly beaten
salt and pepper

Preheat the grill to high. Grill the bacon until crisp. Allow to cool slightly, then cut into small pieces and set aside.

Heat the oil in a large heavy-based, ovenproof frying pan, add the onion and sauté for 5 minutes, or until softened and tender, stirring occasionally.

Add the potatoes and cook for a further 5 minutes, or until golden, stirring to prevent them sticking to the pan. Add the bacon pieces and peas, and spread the mixture evenly over the base of the pan.

Reheat the grill to high. Season the beaten eggs, then pour them carefully over the onion and potato mixture. Cook over a moderate heat for 5–6 minutes, or until the eggs are just set and the base of the frittata is lightly golden brown.

Place the pan under the grill and cook the top for 3 minutes, or until set and lightly golden. Serve the frittata warm or cold, cut into wedges or fingers.

Sausage & Bean Casserole

serves 4

1 tbsp olive oil

8 lean pork sausages

1 onion, finely chopped

1 red pepper, deseeded and chopped

6 tomatoes, deseeded and chopped

1.2 kg / 2 lb 10 oz canned no-salt-added
  mixed pulses, drained

600 ml / 1 pint passata

1 tbsp chopped fresh parsley

1 tbsp tomato purée

salt and pepper

3 tbsp natural yogurt (optional)

Preheat the oven to 180°C/350°F/Gas Mark 4. Heat the oil in a non-stick frying pan and briefly brown the sausages. Remove from the pan with a slotted spoon and drain on kitchen paper. Add the onion and red pepper to the frying pan and cook until soft, then add the tomatoes and simmer for a further 2–3 minutes.

Add the pulses, passata, parsley, tomato purée and salt and pepper to taste and cook for 5 minutes.

Spoon the pulses and sauce into a casserole dish and add the sausages. Cover and cook in the preheated oven for 25 minutes.

Remove from the oven and serve hot with a swirl of yogurt, if liked.

Pizza Fingers

serves 2

pizza base

225 g / 8 oz strong white flour, sifted

1 tsp salt

½ tsp easy-blend yeast

150 ml / 5 fl oz warm water

1 tbsp olive oil

tomato sauce

2 tsp olive oil, plus extra for greasing
    and sprinkling

1 garlic clove, crushed

140 g / 5 oz passata

½ tsp sugar

½ tsp dried oregano

salt and pepper

toppings

handful of cooked fresh spinach leaves,
    tough stalks removed, shredded and
    squeezed dry

75 g / 2¼ oz canned tuna in oil, drained

½ yellow or orange pepper, deseeded and
    finely sliced

4 slices salami

115 g / 4 oz mozzarella cheese

85 g / 3 oz Cheddar cheese, grated

To make the pizza base, place the flour, salt and yeast in a bowl. Make a well in the centre of the flour and add the water and oil, then mix with a knife until the mixture forms a soft dough.

Turn out onto a lightly floured work surface and knead for 5 minutes. Cover and leave for 5 minutes. Knead again for a further 5 minutes until the dough is elastic. Place in a lightly oiled bowl and cover with clingfilm. Leave in a warm place for 45 minutes or until doubled in size.

Preheat the oven to 220°C/425°F/Gas Mark 7. To make the tomato sauce, heat the oil in a heavy-based frying pan and fry the garlic for 1 minute, or until softened. Add the passata and sugar, then cook for 5–7 minutes, until reduced and thickened. Stir in the oregano and seasoning, then set aside.

Knead the risen dough lightly, then roll out to form a rough rectangle and place in an oiled rectangular tin. If you are not using a tin, place the base on a lightly oiled baking sheet and push up the edges of the dough to form a shallow rim.

Spoon the tomato mixture over the base. Top one quarter of the base with the cooked spinach, a second quarter with tuna, a third quarter with the yellow pepper and the remaining quarter with salami. Break the mozzarella cheese with your fingers and sprinkle it over the toppings. Sprinkle over the Cheddar cheese. Season and drizzle with a little olive oil.

Bake in the top of the oven for 12–15 minutes, until the topping is slightly crisp and golden. Slice into fingers before serving.

Home-made Fish Fingers & Sweet Potato Wedges

makes 8–10 fingers

*280 g / 10 oz thick cod fillets, skin and
    bones removed*

flour, for dusting

1 tsp paprika

salt and pepper

*fresh breadcrumbs or fine cornmeal,
    for coating*

1 egg, beaten

sunflower oil, for frying

fresh peas or frozen pears, cooked, to serve

sweet potato wedges

*450 g / 1 lb sweet potatoes, scrubbed and
    cut into wedges*

1 tbsp olive oil

To make the potato wedges, preheat the oven to 200°C/400°F/Gas Mark 6.

Dry the sweet potato wedges on a clean tea towel. Place the oil in a roasting tin and heat for a few minutes in the oven. Arrange the potatoes in the tin and bake for 30–35 minutes, turning them halfway through, until tender and golden.

Meanwhile, cut the cod into strips about 2 cm / $^3/4$ inch wide.

Put the flour onto a plate, add the paprika and season to taste. Put the breadcrumbs onto a second plate. Roll the cod strips in the seasoned flour until coated, shaking off any excess, then dip them in the beaten egg. Roll the cod strips in the breadcrumbs until evenly coated.

Heat enough oil to cover the base of a large, non-stick frying pan. Carefully arrange the fish fingers in the pan – you may have to cook them in batches – and fry them for 3–4 minutes on each side or until crisp and golden. Drain on kitchen paper before serving, if necessary.

Serve the fish fingers with the sweet potato wedges and peas.

Salmon Fishcakes

makes 12

700 g / 1 lb 9 oz skinless salmon fillet,
    cut into cubes
300 ml / 10 fl oz milk
1 bay leaf
100 g / 3½ oz broccoli, steamed until
    tender
700 g / 1 lb 9 oz potatoes, boiled and
    mashed
2 tbsp finely chopped fresh parsley
4 tbsp wholemeal plain flour
pepper
1 egg yolk
2 large eggs, beaten
150 g / 5½ oz fresh wholemeal
    breadcrumbs
2 tbsp olive oil

Preheat the oven to 200°C/400°F/Gas Mark 6. Put the salmon in a saucepan with the milk and bay leaf and bring slowly up to simmering point. Simmer for 2 minutes, then remove the saucepan from the heat, lift out and discard the bay leaf and leave the fish in the milk to cool. When cool, lift out the fish with a slotted spoon and place on kitchen paper to drain.

Flake the fish into a large bowl. Put the broccoli in a food processor and pulse until smooth. Add to the fish with the mashed potatoes, the parsley, 1 tablespoon of the flour, and pepper to taste. Add the egg yolk and mix well. If the mixture is a little dry, add some of the poaching milk; if too wet, add a little more flour.

Divide the mixture into 12 portions and shape each portion into a cake. Put the beaten eggs, remaining flour and the breadcrumbs on 3 separate plates. Roll each fishcake in the flour, then in the beaten egg, and then in the breadcrumbs to coat.

Heat the oil in a non-stick baking tin in the preheated oven for 5 minutes. Add the fishcakes and bake for 10 minutes, then carefully turn the fishcakes over and bake for a further 10 minutes.

chapter 3

Vegetable Delights

Roast Vegetable Lasagne

serves 4

3 tbsp olive oil

4 courgettes, halved lengthways and
    thickly sliced

3 red peppers, deseeded and chopped

1 aubergine, chopped

2 red onions, chopped

5 shallots, peeled and quartered

250 g / 9 oz button mushrooms

400 g / 14 oz canned chopped tomatoes

1 tbsp tomato purée

50 g / 1¼ oz butter

50 g / 1¼ oz plain flour

600 ml / 1 pint milk

salt and pepper

100 g / 3½ oz Cheddar cheese, grated

200 g / 7 oz fresh lasagne

2 tbsp grated Parmesan cheese

Preheat the oven to 190°C/375°F/Gas Mark 5. Put the oil in a large bowl, add the courgettes, peppers, aubergine, onions and shallots and toss well to coat.

Divide the vegetables between 2 baking trays and roast in the preheated oven for 30–40 minutes until soft and flecked with brown. Add the button mushrooms after 20 minutes.

Remove the vegetables from the oven and tip into a large bowl. Add the tomatoes and tomato purée and mix well.

Melt the butter in a saucepan over a low heat. Stir in the flour and cook, stirring constantly, for 2–3 minutes. Gradually add the milk and cook, continuing to stir constantly, until the sauce is thick and smooth. Season to taste with salt and pepper and stir in the Cheddar cheese.

Layer the vegetable mixture and sauce in an ovenproof dish with the lasagne, finishing with a layer of sauce. Sprinkle over the Parmesan cheese and bake in the oven for 30–35 minutes.

Remove from the oven and serve hot.

Spanish Omelette

serves 6

200 g / 7 oz new potatoes

1 tbsp olive oil

1 onion, thinly sliced

1 red pepper, deseeded and thinly sliced

2 tomatoes, peeled, deseeded and chopped

6 large eggs

1 tbsp milk

2 tbsp finely grated Parmesan cheese

salt and pepper

Cook the potatoes in a saucepan of boiling water for 8–12 minutes until tender. Drain and leave to cool, then slice.

Heat the oil in an 18–20-cm/7–8-inch frying pan with a heatproof handle and cook the sliced onion and red pepper until soft. Add the tomatoes and cook for a further minute.

Add the potatoes to the pan and spread out evenly. Beat the eggs, milk, cheese and salt and pepper to taste in a bowl and pour over the potato mixture. Cook for 4–5 minutes until the eggs are set underneath.

Meanwhile, preheat the grill to high. Place the frying pan under the grill and cook the omelette for a further 3–4 minutes until the eggs are set completely.

Leave to cool, then cut into wedges.

Spicy Rice Balls with Tomato Sauce

serves 4

85 g / 3 oz arborio rice

300 ml / 10 fl oz vegetable stock

1 tbsp olive oil

1 onion, finely chopped

2 garlic cloves, finely chopped

1 tsp ground cumin

1 tsp ground coriander

¹/₂ tsp paprika

*200 g / 7 oz canned chickpeas, drained
    and rinsed*

1 egg, beaten

fine cornmeal or polenta, for coating

3–4 tbsp sesame seeds

sunflower oil, for frying

tomato sauce

1 tbsp olive oil

1 garlic clove, finely chopped

400 g / 14 oz passata

2 tsp tomato purée

¹/₂ tsp sugar

salt and pepper

Place the rice in a saucepan and cover with the stock, stirring well. Bring to the boil, then reduce the heat and simmer, covered, for 15–20 minutes, or until the water has been absorbed and the rice is tender. Remove from the heat, cover and let stand for 5 minutes. Drain and cool.

To make the tomato sauce, heat the oil in a heavy-based saucepan and sauté the garlic for 1 minute or until softened. Reduce the heat, add the passata, purée and sugar and season to taste. Cook until the sauce has reduced and thickened, then keep warm.

Meanwhile, make the rice balls. Heat the olive oil in a heavy-based frying pan. Add the onion and fry until softened. Add the garlic and spices and cook for 1 minute, stirring. Stir in the rice, chickpeas and the beaten egg. Transfer the mixture to a food processor and process until fairly smooth. Season to taste.

Put the cornmeal and sesame seeds onto a plate. Form all the mixture into walnut-sized balls and roll in the cornmeal and sesame seeds. Heat enough oil in a frying pan to cover its base and add the rice balls. Cook for 4 minutes, or until crisp and golden, turning occasionally. (You will have to cook the balls in batches.) Drain the rice balls on kitchen paper to mop up any excess oil. Serve immediately with the warm tomato sauce.

Bean Burgers

makes 6

400 g / 14 oz canned cannellini beans,
    drained and rinsed

2 tbsp red pesto

75 g / 2¼ oz fresh wholemeal
    breadcrumbs

1 egg

salt and pepper

2 tbsp olive oil

½ small red onion, finely chopped

1 garlic clove, crushed

6 Granary rolls

6 tsp hummus (see page 24)

2 cherry tomatoes, sliced, to serve

cucumber, sliced, to serve

green salad leaves, to serve

Using a potato masher, mash the beans in a bowl until they are smooth, then add the pesto, breadcrumbs, egg, a pinch of salt and pepper, to taste, and mix well.

Heat half the oil in a non-stick frying pan over a low heat and cook the onion and garlic until soft. Add to the bean mixture and mix well.

Heat the remaining oil in the frying pan. Spoon in the bean mixture, in 6 separate mounds, then press each one down with the back of a spoon to form a burger.

Cook the burgers for 4–5 minutes, then carefully turn over and cook for a further 4–5 minutes until golden.

Meanwhile, slice the rolls in half and smear each one with the hummus.

Remove the burgers from the frying pan and drain on kitchen paper. Place each one in a roll, top with the tomatoes, cucumber and salad leaves and serve.

Easy Scone Pizzas

serves 6

2 tbsp olive oil, plus extra for oiling

1 onion, chopped

800 g / 1 lb 12 oz canned chopped
tomatoes, drained

1 tsp tomato purée

1 tbsp fresh thyme leaves

pepper

1 red pepper, deseeded and thinly sliced

1 yellow pepper, deseeded and thinly sliced

1 courgette, thinly sliced

250 g / 9 oz baby spinach leaves

200 g / 7 oz wholemeal plain flour

250 g / 9 oz white plain flour, plus extra
for dusting

1 tsp demerara sugar

1 tsp bicarbonate of soda

1 tsp sea salt

350 ml / 12 fl oz buttermilk

3 slices ham (optional), chopped

250 g / 9 oz mozzarella, thinly sliced

Heat half the oil in a large frying pan and cook the onion for 5 minutes until soft but not browned. Add the tomatoes, tomato purée and thyme and season to taste with pepper. Simmer for 30 minutes until you have a thick sauce with almost no liquid. Remove from the frying pan and leave to cool.

Heat the remaining oil in the frying pan and cook the peppers and courgette for 5–8 minutes until just beginning to brown. Leave to cool.

Steam the spinach for 3 minutes or until tender. Squeeze out any excess water and chop.

Preheat the oven to 220°C/425°F/Gas Mark 7. Lightly oil 2 baking sheets. Put the flours, sugar, bicarbonate of soda and salt in a large bowl, add the buttermilk and mix well to form a dough. Turn out onto a floured work surface and knead briefly.

Divide the dough into 6 pieces, roll out each piece into a 13-cm/5-inch round and place on the prepared baking sheets. Spread the pizza bases with the tomato sauce, then top with the spinach, peppers, courgette, ham, if using and cheese. Bake in the preheated oven for 25 minutes.

Remove from the oven and serve.

Crispy Vegetable Bake

serves 4

25 g / 1 oz butter, plus extra for greasing

750 g / 1 lb 10 oz potatoes, thinly sliced

3 tbsp olive oil

1 garlic clove, crushed

1 tsp fresh oregano leaves

1 large leek, shredded

2 parsnips, peeled and grated

3 carrots, peeled and grated

½ head celeriac, peeled and grated

salt and pepper

200 g / 7 oz feta cheese, crumbled

4 eggs

Preheat the oven to 190°C/375°F/Gas Mark 5. Grease a 20-cm/8-inch round baking dish with butter.

Cook the potato slices in a large saucepan of boiling water for 5 minutes. Drain and cover with a clean tea towel to absorb the steam.

Melt half the butter with 1 tablespoon of the oil in a large frying pan and cook the garlic, oregano and leek for 3–4 minutes. Remove with a slotted spoon and transfer to a plate. Add the remaining oil to the frying pan and cook the parsnips, carrots and celeriac for 10 minutes until soft and cooked through. Season to taste with salt and pepper and cook for a further 5 minutes. Stir in the leek mixture.

Arrange half the potato slices in the bottom of the prepared dish, top with half the vegetable mixture and then sprinkle over half the cheese. Cover with the remaining vegetable mixture and cheese and top with the remaining potato slices. Dot with the remaining butter and bake in the preheated oven for 40 minutes until golden and crisp.

Five minutes before serving, poach the eggs. Serve the vegetable bake topped with the poached eggs.

Pesto Potatoes

makes 1 portion

1 small baking potato, scrubbed
handful of spinach leaves, shredded
1 tbsp freshly grated Cheddar or
  Parmesan cheese

pesto

25 g / 1 oz fresh basil leaves
1 garlic clove, crushed
15 g / ¼ oz pine kernels
4 tbsp olive oil
2 tbsp freshly grated Parmesan cheese

Preheat the oven to 200°C/400°F/Gas Mark 6. Bake the potato for 1–1½ hours, until tender.

To make the pesto, place the basil, garlic and pine kernels in a blender and process until finely chopped. Gradually add the olive oil and then the Parmesan cheese and blend to a coarse purée.

Steam the spinach for 3 minutes, or until tender. Squeeze out any excess water and chop. Preheat the grill to high.

Cut the potato in half and scoop out most of the flesh, reserving the skins. Put the potato flesh in a bowl with 2 tablespoons of pesto and the spinach and mash until combined. Spoon the pesto and potato mixture back into the potato skins and sprinkle with the Cheddar cheese.

Place the potatoes under a hot grill for a minute or two until the cheese is bubbling and golden.

Bubble & Squeak Patties

serves 4

*700 g / 1 lb 9 oz potatoes, peeled and
   cut into even-sized pieces*
*300 g / 10½ oz Savoy or green cabbage,
   finely shredded*
1 tbsp olive oil
1 onion, finely chopped
1 tsp Dijon mustard
85 g / 3 oz mature Cheddar cheese, grated
1 egg, beaten
salt and pepper
flour, for dusting
vegetable oil, for frying

Cook the potatoes in salted boiling water for 15 minutes, or until tender.
Drain well.

Meanwhile, steam the cabbage for 5–8 minutes, or until tender.

While the potatoes and cabbage are cooking, heat the oil in a heavy-based
frying pan. Fry the onion for 5–8 minutes.

Place the potatoes and cabbage in a large bowl and mash using a potato
masher. Add the onion, mustard, Cheddar, egg and seasoning and mix
well with a wooden spoon until all the ingredients are combined. Leave
until cool enough to handle.

Flour a large plate and your hands and shape the mixture into 8 patties.
Heat enough oil to cover the base of a large frying pan and fry the patties
in batches over a medium heat for 3–4 minutes on each side. Serve
immediately.

Creamy Pasta Bake

serves 4

175 g/6 oz wholewheat pasta shells
1 tbsp olive oil
125 g/4½ oz button mushrooms, quartered
1 broccoli head, broken into small florets
1 tbsp cornflour
200 ml/7 fl oz milk
125 ml/4 fl oz half-fat crème fraîche
salt and pepper
50 g/1¼ oz Cheddar cheese, grated

Preheat the oven to 190°C/375°F/Gas Mark 5. Cook the wholewheat pasta shells in a large saucepan of boiling water for 10–12 minutes until just tender, then drain.

Meanwhile, heat the oil in a large frying pan and cook the mushrooms until beginning to brown. Boil or steam the broccoli until just cooked, then drain.

Blend the cornflour with a little milk in a jug, then gradually add the remaining milk, stirring constantly. Pour into the pan, add the crème fraîche and warm through, stirring.

Add the pasta and broccoli to the frying pan and season to taste with salt and pepper. Mix well, then transfer to a baking dish, top with the cheese and bake in the preheated oven for 15 minutes. Serve hot.

Chinese Noodles

serves 4

250 g pack of tofu, drained and cubed

salt

250 g/9 oz medium egg noodles

1 tbsp peanut or vegetable oil

1 red pepper, deseeded and sliced

225 g/8 oz broccoli florets

175 g/6 oz baby sweetcorn, halved
  lengthways

2–3 tbsp water

2 spring onions, finely sliced

1 tbsp sesame seeds, toasted (optional)

marinade

1 garlic clove, finely chopped

2.5-cm/1-inch piece fresh root ginger,
  peeled and grated

1 tsp sesame oil

1 tbsp runny honey

2 tbsp dark soy sauce

Mix together the ingredients for the marinade in a shallow dish. Add the tofu and spoon the marinade over. Refrigerate for 1 hour to marinate, turning the tofu occasionally to allow the flavours to infuse.

Preheat the oven to 200°C/400°F/Gas Mark 6. Using a slotted spoon, remove the tofu from the marinade and reserve the liquid. Arrange the tofu on a baking sheet and roast for 20 minutes, turning occasionally, until the tofu pieces are golden and crisp on all sides.

Meanwhile, cook the noodles in plenty of salted boiling water according to the instructions on the packet, until the noodles are tender, then drain. Rinse the noodles under cold running water and drain again.

Heat a wok or heavy-based frying pan, then add the oil. Add the pepper, broccoli and sweetcorn and stir-fry, tossing and stirring continuously, over a medium-high heat for 5–8 minutes or until the vegetables have softened. Add the water and continue to stir-fry until the vegetables are just tender but remain slightly crunchy.

Stir in the marinade, noodles, tofu and spring onions and stir-fry until heated through. Serve sprinkled with sesame seeds, if using.

chapter 4

Sweet Endings

Apricot & Sunflower Seed Cookies

makes 20

100 g / 3½ oz unsalted butter, softened

50 g / 1¼ oz demerara sugar

1 tbsp maple syrup

1 tbsp honey, plus extra for brushing

1 large egg, beaten

100 g / 3½ oz white plain flour,
    plus extra for dusting

150 g / 5½ oz wholemeal plain flour

1 tbsp oat bran

50 g / 1¼ oz ground almonds

1 tsp ground cinnamon

75 g / 2¼ oz ready-to-eat dried apricots,
    chopped

25 g / 1 oz sunflower seeds

Beat the softened butter with the sugar in a large bowl until light and fluffy. Beat in the maple syrup and honey, then the egg.

Add the flours and oat bran, then the almonds and mix well. Add the cinnamon, apricots and seeds and, with floured hands, mix to a firm dough. Wrap in clingfilm and chill for 30 minutes.

Preheat the oven to 180°C/350°F/Gas Mark 4. Roll out the dough on a lightly floured work surface to 1 cm/½ inch thick. Using a 6-cm/2½-inch biscuit cutter, cut out 20 rounds, re-rolling the trimmings where possible, and place on a baking sheet. Brush with a little extra honey and bake in the preheated oven for 15 minutes until golden. Remove from the oven and leave to cool on a wire rack.

Orange & Banana Scones

makes 12

sunflower oil, for oiling

150 g / 5½ oz white self-raising flour,
    plus extra for dusting, and for rolling
    if needed

150 g / 5½ oz light brown self-raising
    flour

1 tsp baking powder

½ tsp ground cinnamon

75 g / 2¾ oz unsalted butter, diced
    and chilled

50 g / 1¾ oz demerara sugar

150 ml / 5 fl oz milk, plus extra for
    brushing

1 ripe banana, peeled and mashed

finely grated rind of 1 orange

150 g / 5½ oz fresh raspberries, lightly
    mashed

Preheat the oven to 200°C / 400°F / Gas Mark 6. Lightly oil a baking sheet.

Mix the flours, baking powder and cinnamon together in a large bowl, add the butter and rub in with your fingertips until the mixture resembles breadcrumbs. Stir in the sugar. Make a well in the middle and pour in the milk, add the banana and orange rind and mix to a soft dough. The dough will be quite wet.

Turn out the dough onto a lightly floured work surface and, adding a little more flour if needed, roll out to 2 cm / ³/4 inch thick. Using a 6-cm / 2¹/2-inch biscuit cutter, cut out 12 scones, re-rolling the trimmings where possible, and place them on the prepared baking sheet. Brush with milk and bake in the preheated oven for 10–12 minutes.

Remove from the oven and leave to cool slightly, then halve the scones and fill with the raspberries.

Gingerbread People

makes 6 people or more, depending on the size of the cutter

175 g / 6 oz plain flour

2 tsp ground ginger

½ tsp bicarbonate of soda

55 g / 2 oz butter or margarine

85 g / 3 oz soft brown sugar

2 tbsp golden syrup

1 egg, beaten

to decorate

Smarties and jelly orange and lemon cake decorations

Preheat the oven to 190°C/375°F/Gas Mark 5. Sift the flour, ginger and bicarbonate of soda into a large mixing bowl. Add the butter and rub into the flour with your fingertips until it resembles fine breadcrumbs. Mix in the sugar.

Warm the syrup in a small saucepan until runny, then add to the flour mixture with the beaten egg. Mix to form a soft dough, then knead lightly until smooth. If the dough is too sticky, add a little extra flour.

Roll out the dough on a lightly floured work surface then, using a cutter, make the gingerbread people. Place on a lightly greased baking sheet and cook for 10 minutes, or until just crisp and golden. Allow to cool.

Use the Smarties to make eyes and buttons, and attach the jelly orange and lemon cake decorations to make a mouth.

Chocolate Mousse Pots

makes 6

100 g / 3½ oz plain chocolate (minimum
    70% cocoa solids), chopped

1 tbsp butter

2 large eggs, separated

1 tbsp maple syrup

2 tbsp Greek-style yogurt

100 g / 3½ oz blueberries

1 tbsp water

25 g / 1 oz white chocolate, grated

Put the chocolate and butter in a heatproof bowl, set the bowl over a saucepan of barely simmering water and heat until melted. Leave to cool slightly, then stir in the egg yolks, maple syrup and yogurt.

Whisk the egg whites in a large, grease-free bowl until stiff, then fold into the chocolate mixture. Divide between 6 small ramekins and chill for 4 hours.

Meanwhile, put the blueberries in a small saucepan with the water and cook until the berries begin to pop and turn glossy. Leave to cool, then chill.

To serve, top each mousse with a few blueberries and a little white chocolate.

Blueberry Bran Muffins

makes 10

150 g / 5½ oz white plain flour

100 g / 3½ oz light brown self-raising
  flour

1 tbsp oat bran

2 tsp baking powder

½ tsp bicarbonate of soda

pinch of salt

50 g / 1¾ oz demerara sugar

1 tbsp clear honey

1 large egg

200 ml / 7 fl oz buttermilk

150 g / 5½ oz fresh blueberries

Preheat the oven to 180°C/350°F/Gas Mark 4. Line 10 holes of a muffin tin with muffin paper cases.

Mix the flours, bran, baking powder, bicarbonate of soda and salt together in a bowl and stir in the sugar. Whisk the honey, egg and buttermilk together in a jug.

Pour the wet ingredients into the dry and stir briefly to combine. Don't overmix – the mixture should still be a little lumpy. Fold in the blueberries.

Spoon the mixture into the paper cases and bake in the preheated oven for 20 minutes until risen and lightly browned.

Remove the muffins from the oven and leave to cool in the tin. Serve warm or cold.

Mini Strawberry Cheesecakes

makes 6

75 g / 2¾ oz unsalted butter
75 g / 2¾ oz rolled oats
25 g / 1 oz chopped hazelnuts
225 g / 8 oz ricotta cheese
50 g / 1¾ oz demerara sugar
finely grated rind of 1 lemon, and
juice of ½ lemon
1 egg, plus 1 egg yolk
150 g / 5½ oz cottage cheese
1 kiwi fruit
6 large strawberries

Line 6 holes of a muffin tin with muffin paper cases.

Melt the butter in a small saucepan over a low heat, then leave to cool. Put the oats in a food processor and pulse briefly to break them up, then tip into a bowl, add the nuts and melted butter and mix well. Divide the mixture between the paper cases and press down well. Chill for 30 minutes.

Preheat the oven to 150°C/300°F/Gas Mark 2. Beat the ricotta cheese with the sugar, and lemon rind and juice, in a bowl. Add the egg, egg yolk and cottage cheese and mix well. Spoon into the muffin cases and bake in the preheated oven for 30 minutes. Turn off the oven, but leave the cheesecakes in the oven until completely cold.

Peel the kiwi fruit and slice the flesh, and half the strawberries. Remove the paper cases, top each cheesecake with the fruit and serve.

Cereal Fruit Cupcakes

makes 12

100 g / 3½ oz unsalted butter

125 g / 4½ oz clear honey

150 g / 5½ oz porridge oats

50 g / 1¼ oz unsweetened crispy rice

1 tbsp sesame seeds

100 g / 3½ oz mixed dried fruit, such
as pears, mangos, apples and
cranberries, chopped

50 g / 1¼ oz shelled pecan nuts, chopped

Melt the butter and honey in a small saucepan over a low heat.

Mix the oats, crispy rice, sesame seeds, dried fruit and chopped nuts together in a bowl, add the melted butter and honey and stir to combine.

Spoon into 12 paper cake cases and press down well. Chill for 6 hours before serving.

Ice Cream Strawberry Sundae

serves 4

8 scoops of good-quality
    vanilla ice cream
25 g / 1 oz chopped mixed nuts, lightly
    toasted in a dry frying pan
grated chocolate and marshmallows,
    to serve

strawberry sauce

250 g / 9 oz strawberries, hulled and
    halved
2 tbsp freshly squeezed orange juice
2 tbsp caster sugar

To make the sauce, put the strawberries in a blender with the orange juice and process until smooth. Transfer the mixture to a saucepan and add the sugar. Cook over a medium heat for 10–12 minutes, or until thickened. Leave to cool.

To serve, place a spoonful of the strawberry sauce in the bottom of a tall glass. Add two scoops of ice cream and another spoonful of fruit sauce. Sprinkle with the nuts and chocolate. Arrange the marshmallows on top. Repeat to make four sundaes.

Sticky Fruit Flapjacks

makes 16

175 g/6 oz unsalted butter, plus extra
    for greasing
3 tbsp clear honey
150 g/5½ oz demerara sugar
100 g/3½ oz no-added-sugar smooth
    peanut butter
225 g/8 oz porridge oats
50 g/1¾ oz ready-to-eat dried apricots,
    chopped
2 tbsp sunflower seeds
2 tbsp sesame seeds

Preheat the oven to 180°C/350°F/Gas Mark 4. Grease and line a 22-cm/8½-inch square baking tin.

Melt the butter, honey and sugar in a saucepan over a low heat. When the sugar has melted, add the peanut butter and stir until all the ingredients are well combined. Add all the remaining ingredients and mix well.

Press the mixture into the prepared tin and bake in the preheated oven for 20 minutes.

Remove from the oven and leave to cool in the tin, then cut into 16 squares.

Fruit Skewers

makes 4

selection of fruit, such as apricots,
    peaches, figs, strawberries, mangoes,
    pineapple, bananas, dates and
    pawpaw, prepared and cut into chunks
maple syrup
50 g/1¼ oz plain chocolate (minimum
    70% cocoa solids), broken into chunks

Soak 4 bamboo skewers in water for at least 20 minutes.

Preheat the grill to high and line the grill pan with foil. Thread pieces of fruit onto each skewer. Brush the fruit with a little maple syrup.

Put the chocolate in a heatproof bowl, set the bowl over a saucepan of barely simmering water and heat until it is melted.

Meanwhile, cook the skewers under the preheated grill for 3 minutes, or until caramelized. Serve drizzled with a little of the melted chocolate, removing the fruit from the skewer if serving to younger children.